THE ART OF ADDICTION

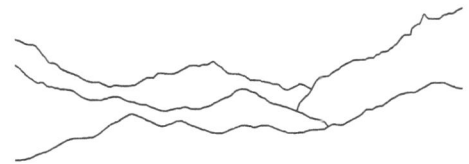

RE-ENVISIONING ADDICTION'S ROLE IN OUR LIVES

Nicole Daedone
with Kate Feigin

soulmaker | PRESS

soulmaker | PRESS

soulmakerpress.com

ISBN: 978-1-961064-21-8

CONTENTS

OVERVIEW

The Art of Addiction is a step workbook that paints a bold, revolutionary portrait of addiction, one that focuses on the lessons, messages, and gifts of addiction, not the shame. In this curriculum we learn not to judge the experience but to embrace it for what it offers us: creativity, desire, drive, and access to the flow of life.

In this workbook there are eight lessons. Each lesson includes a meditation and journal exercises. Some also include additional exercises. There is space after each exercise for your response. You may also use the space in the margins to write any notes or additional thoughts. If you choose to revisit the questions and prompts at a later time (which is highly recommended), you may answer the questions in a separate journal.

KEY TERMS

Soul: Soul is the deepest, most complex part of ourself. It is our essence and is unique to us. It is dynamic, navigates both the light and the dark, and influences our lives regardless of our awareness. Our creativity, desire, and genius come from our soul. Our soul wants to express itself and our inner vitality. It encompasses hidden aspects of ourself, including parts of ourself we may try to not acknowledge (like our shadow parts).

Obsession: Obsession is a state we may find ourself in where our mind is intensely focused in a single direction: on a particular object, idea, activity, or person. Our attention and energy are hyper-focused. Being in the state of obsession can lead to addiction.

Calling: Our calling is our purpose in life, what we are drawn to, in an almost magnetic way. We are each "called" to express our unique blueprint in this life, our true purpose which is the full expression of our gifts and how we will contribute to the world. In finding, moving toward, and embracing our calling, we become our fullest self.

Possession: Possession occurs when our rational mind is no longer in control of us. We surrender our control and let ourself be taken by something—life, desire, an object, a substance, or a person.

Addiction: Addiction is a conditioned response to bond with something. Addiction is driven by a genius impulse inside of us, looking to express our innate gifts, and often manifests as an intense focus on a particular substance, behavior, activity, or person. Embedded in addiction is a deep-rooted desire for complete dissolving of ourself.

"*An addiction (a repetitious act) is a ritual to help one through a trying time; its repetition safeguards the passage, it becomes one's talisman, one's touchstone.*"

~Gloria Anzaldúa

REHUMANIZATION

LESSON 1

Rehumanization is a transformative process involving three stages: the obsession stage, where we must patiently confront our addictions; the breakdown stage, where we disconnect from old bonds and begin to see a new path; and the re-plugging in stage, where we connect deeply with our inner purpose and contribute uniquely to the world.

What do we mean by "Rehumanization"? We define it as a return to our humanity, a return to our true self, with the layers of shame, doubt, and pain stripped away. When we return to our humanity, we feel deeply connected to the flow of life. We recognize our unique gifts and we are able to access them to contribute to the world. We become whole.

There are three stages to the process of rehumanizing: obsession, breakdown, and re-plugging in.

Stage 1: Obsession Stage

The obsession stage of addiction is almost like an anesthesia that keeps the rational mind "asleep" while the soul travels down to the depths to get its calling and its power.

It is important to note that we cannot be hurried along the process here. We cannot force growth, just like we cannot force a flower bud to open early by prying it apart or it will die. Others might try to drag us along the path, which creates resistance. It is important that anyone on this journey be met wherever they are with compassion and tenderness.

The biggest pitfall in this stage is to try to rush through the cycle to its completion. We must practice patience.

Journal Exercise

- What is your current experience with the obsession stage?

- In your past, when have you had an experience with obsession?

Stage 2: Breakdown Stage

In the breakdown stage, we unplug from what we are bonded to. During this time, we dry out. We are in a challenging limbo-like space between death and rebirth. We either go forward into a new place or back to complete what was incomplete in the obsession stage. At this moment, it's a tug of war. The pull toward our new reality needs to be just a little stronger than the pull back to our old reality. In that small space, perhaps a sliver of light through a door, we see creativity begin to blossom. We see a power and a determination to move forward along this new path.

In this stage, we notice a natural rise in our resourcefulness. Obsession orders our mind in a single direction. We only focus on what we are obsessed with or addicted to. This is the training of hyper-focus. Obsession creates the pathways we need later on. When the obsession stage is truly complete, we feel discomfort, but the relief we feel outweighs the discomfort. If the relief does not outweigh the discomfort, the obsession stage was disrupted by self-will and we will return to stage one because it isn't truly complete. The question we ask in this stage: Is there more relief or more agitation, more letting go or more restricted control? If there is a "Thank God," we have truly made it into stage two.

Journal Exercise

- What is your current experience with the breakdown stage?

- What is a moment in your past when you have had an experience with breaking down?

Stage 2: Breakdown Stage (continued)

At some point, things become clear. We get our internal "marching orders" and we start to move according to a deeper vision. Confusion is replaced with conviction as we now have access to our soul's direction. The feeling of being lost is gone, because the question of, "What am I here to do?" has been answered.

Our identity begins to form around this vision and understanding. We are called to go deeper. We feel as if there is a magnet drawing in some things and repelling others. The duty has been transformed into devotion to the soul. We answer to this first and accept guidance that will support this development.

This is a tricky process. If it's not the right time for us to be in the breakdown stage, because we are not done with the obsession stage, or because it is not done well, we are a live wire. We will waste all the energy and return to obsession more passionately in order to find the calm of an ordered mind. The obsession or addiction becomes stronger.

We can't will ourselves through this stage. It can only happen when we have truly completed the obsession stage, when there is no more juice left in the obsession.

Stage 3: Re-plugging In

The final stage is re-plugging in. We bond with something new with the same level of intensity and obsession we had in stage one. However, the obsession shifts from reaching outside of ourselves to reaching down and inside ourselves. This is a type of possession, being inhabited by the force that animates all of life. We are possessed by our calling, our purpose in life. We feel rooted and connected to humanity.

In stage three, we become a person unto ourselves, a "lighthouse." We find our own place within the system we live. Our purpose, our calling, is unique to us. We are specialists in something and everything galvanizes around that. We are connected in the larger flow of life, open, now that we are not in a closed obsession stage, so what we are doing can flow out and what we need can flow in. We become connected, as if we are synapses in the nervous system of the planet.

From here, we do two main things for the rest of our lives. First, we do this procedure over and over at more subtle levels to reconcentrate the magnet within us. This keeps us humble too, because we are always in this process, repeating it in various areas of our life. Second, we offer our unique calling to the world, securing our connection to life.

In the previous stage, we got our marching orders. Now we must perfect them. We interact with that which is around us, always listening and tending to. We move forward with joy, without fear of falling back. We move forward with a fuller awareness and trust.

Journal Exercise

- What is your current experience with the re-plugging in stage?

- What is a moment in your past when you had an experience with plugging in?

Meditation: Here You Are

Take a deep breath and notice how you feel in your body and how the world around you feels.

Take another breath for the day you've had so far.

Take a breath for this precious moment, which cannot be recreated.

Now another for the day and night that is coming.

Here you are, in the cycle between past and future, choosing to spend your miraculous time in the exploration of how humans can find liberation from addiction while incarcerated. Here you are shaping change through community.

Addiction can be a heavy topic. It can be a source of sorrow and pain. We are here today to notice how our small collective actions can create an ecosystem of care that will benefit many of those still on the inside.

We are here to intentionally grow our capacity to embody the worlds we long for, or longed for while incarcerated. We are here to stoke the embers, blowing tenderly upon them until they become steady, unwavering flames. We are the keepers of this fire.

Integration Exercise

- Journal about what it means for you to live in the idea cf Rehumanization.

- How will you live your life from this place?

- What would it look like and feel like?

- How could you be the face of love in the world?

"Out beyond ideas of wrongdoing and rightdoing there is a field. I'll meet you there. When the soul lies down in that grass the world is too full to talk about."

~Rumi

A PATH TO LIBERATION

LESSON 2

We present a controversial perspective on addiction, suggesting it can be a path to spiritual liberation and deep self-connection, challenging the traditional view of addiction as a negative force to be controlled.

I n the last module, we began to explore the idea that addiction is a path unto itself. Addiction is not something to be avoided or denied, like a disease, but is genuinely a path of liberation. Likely, you have never heard addiction spoken about like this before. This course will require opening up to seeing things in an entirely new way. It's up to you to explore it, see if it's true for you, and feel if it resonates.

One important clarification is that addiction can take many forms. Addiction is anything—substances, internet addiction, work addiction, codependency, etc.—that takes you out of control and into the impulses of the body. You are called to it for a reason. Addiction is calling us to embrace the essence and totality of life—ALL of it.

The cultural conversation about addiction is a brutal one. Most of us have known someone or been in this conversation ourselves. Most people have experienced addiction either up close or at a distance. We have been addicted ourselves, have loved addicts, and have felt a level of possession we had never experienced before in the face of it. In this module, we'll learn how this cultural conversation is doing the same thing that the rational part of our mind does to the nonrational part: demonize something it does not understand in an attempt to control or deny it.

The approach to addiction in this course reveals the power that exists inside the experience of it. There is material in this course that might feel like the opposite of everything you believe about addiction. The invitation here is to approach the conversation with a complete beginner's mind. Imagine you're visiting a country you have never been to and know nothing about. Toss

"Around 500 years ago, when the word "addict" entered the English language, it meant something very different: more akin to a "strong devotion." It was something you did, rather than something that happened to you. For example, an early writer counseled his readers to "addict all their doings towards the attainment of life everlasting."

~CARL ERIK FISCHER

out all your previously held beliefs and ideas and see if you can allow yourself to explore with a fresh, open mind, observing, and feeling your way through.

You'll see that the terms "addiction" and "nonrational" are used interchangeably. Our addictive yearning originates from the nonrational part of our being, whereas the voice of logic and reason comes from the rational mind. We need both. The Art of Addiction is about having access to both and about both having a relationship with each other.

The Rational and Nonrational

What if, inside the nonrational part of our mind, exists the template for all spiritual expansion? What if surrendering to it means going inward and stepping outside of the rules of society? What if the nonrational is the fast-track for spiritual adventurers who want to know the whole of life, who want to learn in practice and experience, from the inside out? To be stripped of the pride that makes people feel like they are better than others. What if the nonrational is a calling, and from that calling comes the capacity to truly serve, be able to hear and understand the workings and the whispers of those in pain? Not from a book, not from a distant formula, but from real flesh-and-bone experience.

What if the fear and loathing that accompanies our vices is just the rational mind who views it as a threat to order and control? That it can't stand that no matter what rules it imposes, it is powerless to control this force. So it demonizes it.

The above reading shows the potential for the nonrational as a path for liberation. Addiction has the elements needed: surrender, the willingness to go to great lengths, rejecting what society thinks we should be doing, and creating deep, deep connection with your inner world. These are the same ingredients we use when creating—whether it be solving problems, building houses, or writing poetry—practicing a religion, or meditating.

This path is usually taken by the spiritual adventurers who want a deeper understanding of life. What if we considered that all addicts are really spiritual seekers? Could we be so bold as to question whether the people who have not gone this path are really so much better, or if they just seem safer and more put-together?

This path teaches us to let go of the pride and superiority that come with judgment, opening us up to be more connected with others and the world around us. Addiction has this beautiful way of removing our judgment, superiority, and the sense that we are better than others. When we are humbled by something we really think we should stop doing yet can't seem to stop doing it, suddenly we don't have much of a leg to stand on in judgment of anyone else and how they're living their lives. This can lead us to become a more all-encompassing kind of person who doesn't overlook people from the "world of the below" because we have been there and do not consider ourselves above that place.

Exercise: The Rational and Nonrational Mind

Set up two chairs facing each other. One chair represents your rational mind and the other represents your nonrational mind.

First, sit in the rational mind. Take a moment to drop in. The rational is your rules-and-order mind, right and wrong, control, perfectionism, makes sure you are safe. Embody that persona and let it come to the surface.

Look over to the nonrational "person" in the other chair.

What do you want to say to the nonrational? The part that's feeling lawless and intuitive, that gives freely and has no boundaries. Run through all of the things you want to say.

Once you feel emptied or, if the impulse comes from the nonrational to respond, go over to the other seat.

Sit in the nonrational seat. Drop in, embody that persona, then look over at the rational seat and speak to it.

Continue this exercise. Switching back and forth as you feel the different impulses rise, have them have a conversation with each other. Listen to what the other has to say. Embody the tone, the feeling, the emotions. Is one or the other angry? Fearful? Loving? Hesitant? Shy? Suppressed? Dominant? Sad? Tearful? Allow these feelings to come up naturally.

You may or may not find a resolution. Perhaps it's been so long since they've spoken to each other that there is animosity and anger. Perhaps they are familiar with each other and need to reconnect. Whatever it is, have them listen to each other and find a way to work together for the higher good of the self.

Once the exercise comes to a close, have your rational and nonrational minds thank each other for the conversation.

Sit and meditate for five minutes, integrating the self. Feel your feet on the floor, feel the seat beneath you. Pay attention to your breath. Now, imagine a shower of gold light coming from above and washing over you from head to toe, cleansing your body. When you are ready, open your eyes.

Meditation: Acceptance of All of Our Parts

Find a comfortable place to sit, whether it be somewhere indoors or outside. Take a few minutes to settle into your chair or meditation cushion. Feel your butt on the ground and take some breaths.

Notice any feelings that are arising after the exercise of coming into relationship with your addiction. Do they have a specific location in your body? How do they feel? Are they hot, cold, warm, cool? Do they feel soft or dense, tight or loose?

Allow your mind 2-3 minutes to track and notice, without judgment, the sensations and feelings that are arising. Notice if there's anything that you want to do with the feelings; maybe you want to look away or start fidgeting to move your body. Gently bring your attention back into the feelings at the level of sensation. As you notice the feelings and sensations arising, if you can bring some approval to them, do so.

Allow yourself to return slowly to the room, and when your meditation is done, journal about your experience in your notebook.

Journal Exercise

- What is it like to practice radical acceptance for all of your parts?

*"Where the greatest danger is,
also grows the saving power."*

~Friedrich Hölderlin

ARE CRAVINGS BAD?

LESSON 3

We explore the concept that addiction allows us to experience intense emotions, fostering empathy and compassion, and challenges the stigma and shame associated with addiction. Addiction serves as a nonrational anchor that helps us confront the raw truth of our identities, advocating for the removal of shame to facilitate personal insight and growth.

Wild Geese

> *You do not have to be good.*
> *You do not have to walk on your knees*
> *for a hundred miles through the desert repenting.*
> *You only have to let the soft animal of your body*
> *love what it loves.*
> *Tell me about despair, yours, and I will tell you mine.*
> *Meanwhile the world goes on.*
> *Meanwhile the sun and the clear pebbles of the rain*
> *are moving across the landscapes,*
> *over the prairies and the deep trees,*
> *the mountains and the rivers.*
> *Meanwhile the wild geese, high in the clean blue air,*
> *are heading home again.*
> *Whoever you are, no matter how lonely,*
> *the world offers itself to your imagination,*
> *calls to you like the wild geese, harsh and exciting -*
> *over and over announcing your place*
> *in the family of things.*

~Mary Oliver

We often cast aside the aspects of life that are considered bad, taboo, inappropriate, as well as the behaviors and feelings that are messy—jealousy, rage, lust, grief, and the like. Addiction takes us down into the body where we experience all of these feelings and impulses. By feeling these feelings inside, from our addiction, we develop the capacity for empathy and compassion for others.

There is so much shame and stigma attached to addiction. It's treated like a craving you didn't have enough willpower to steer yourself out of, or something that messed your life up and threw you off the appropriate path you were on. In actuality, the real craving is to be taken out of control. That is why we chose addiction, because of how much we wanted to have this experience.

The rational mind wants to keep our lives ordered and safe, predictable. The nonrational wants us to be actually alive. It provides us with whatever anchor we need to get down into the ground of our lives, the beauty of our body, the grit and truth of who we are. It comes along when we need it and takes us down, where we get to meet ourselves perhaps for the very first time. The rational mind considers this act threatening, and it will use a variety of things to keep us from going there, such as shaming and berating us. It says, "You have a craving you can't control, therefore you are bad, or broken."

One thing this course seeks to do is remove this shame and quiet the berating, so that each person can locate themselves inside whatever addiction experience they're having and let it show them what it's trying to show them. And the thing is, the rational mind doesn't even want to win. It just has to fight until it can let go because that's its nature.

Meditation: The Practice of Getting Curious

Get into a comfortable position, either in a chair or seated on a meditation cushion. Set your timer for 10 minutes. Close your eyes and become aware of your breath and the sensations in your body.

Addiction calls us to know the full range of life. It does not cut any part of ourselves out. In this meditation, allow any thoughts you have to rise to the surface, and say yes to them. Allow them to exist in this space with you.

If you feel doubt, say yes to it. If emotions like boredom, tiredness, anger, or joy rise up, say yes to those emotions and give them a place at the table.

Addiction sees all these thoughts and emotions as part of the beauty of life. See if you can feel the beauty and life force of your thoughts and sensations rise in and out of you like waves in the ocean.

At the end of the meditation, slowly bring yourself back into the room. Feel the seat beneath you and the sounds around you. Gently open your eyes when you are ready. After, journal about your experience in your notebook.

Journal Exercise: Peeling Back the Layers

- Find a comfortable writing place where you can be uninterrupted for ten minutes. As we have read, addiction is a calling to know and experience all aspects of life. Think about a time when you felt a strong craving. Write about how you felt.

- What was truly calling you in that moment? Was it desire? Connection? Love? Escape? Comfort? Excitement? Feel the sensations of that moment in your body—are they hot, cold, warm, or cool? Do you feel chills or are you sweating? Is your body tense or is it soft?

- Write down everything you think and feel.

"Songwriting is about getting the demon out of me. It's like being possessed. You try to go to sleep, but the song won't let you. So you have to get up and make it into something, and then you're allowed to sleep. It's always in the middle of the night, or you're half-awake or tired, when your critical faculties are switched off. So letting go is what the whole game is. Every time you try to put your finger on it, it slips away. You turn on the lights and the cockroaches run away. You can never grasp them..."

~John Lennon

WHAT CALLS YOU?

LESSON 4

Addiction is described as a form of possession that liberates us from our rational constraints, allowing us to fully engage with our impulses and senses. Through the loss of control and the shedding of societal roles, our true self and purpose may be uncovered.

We come to addiction because we want to be possessed. Possession takes us out of our rational mind, where things feel safe and known. It drops us into our impulses where we begin to feel things we may have pushed down or pushed aside. We learn to exist outside of the narrow limitations we set for ourselves and navigate this world with our senses.

Possession teaches us how to see in the dark and make art with our life. It is a total surrender to or an immersion into something, like the way a surfer is taken by the waves or the way a painter is taken by their art. Time and space collapse. In this same way, we can be consumed by the art of using—consumed by how and when to consume and acquire.

Addicts yearn for the deep, the potent, to feel completely taken by something, to feel utterly at one with their present-moment experience that happens in addiction. It is a great friend in this way, as the part of us we can't control keeps pointing to our most intense and powerful desires.

Oftentimes, a calling doesn't reveal itself on the "appropriate trajectory" that we construct for ourselves. It reveals itself when we get knocked down by life, or when we experience a loss of control, or when we are least expecting it. That's when we discover who we are underneath the masks we wear and the roles we play in the day-to-day. All of this falls away, and in the resulting stripped-down-ness of it, it's possible the purpose of *us* is revealed.

Meditation: Feeling Through

Get into a comfortable position, either in a chair or seated on a meditation cushion. Set your timer for 10 minutes. Close your eyes and become aware of your breath and the sensations in your body.

Notice how you feel after the exercise and getting more in touch with a feeling that overtook you. Think about the list you made of things you want to lose.

While you made your list, did you feel grief or sadness? Feel it through. Did you feel relief? Feel that through. Remember, we are only noticing what arises, not trying to change it or judge it. As you sit, notice if there is anything new about yourself. Has anything shifted? Does the sensation in your body feel different? Do you feel differently about the items on your list?

Allow yourself to follow the experience of sensation throughout the meditation, tracking new things that arise. Take a few moments to come out of the meditation, then journal in your notebook about the experience.

Journal Exercise: What Do You Desire to Lose?

■ Make a list of things you would want to lose. For example, you might want to lose some of your pride that prevents you from engaging more with life, set aside ways you relate to people that don't work well, quit a job you hate, or let go of how controlling you are.

■ Write about what you would want to lose and why. How would it make you feel to be without it? What would become possible for you without it?

Know your garden.
It is time to speak your truth.
Create your community.
Be good to each other.
And do not look outside yourself for your leader.

Then he clasped his hands together, smiled, and said,
"This could be a good time! There is a river flowing now
very fast. It is so great and swift that there are those who
will be afraid. They will try to hold on to the shore. They
will feel they are being torn apart and will suffer greatly.
Know the river has its destination. The elders say we
must let go of the shore, push off into the middle of the
river, keep our eyes open, and our heads above the water.

And I say, see who is in there with you and celebrate. At
this time in history, we are to take nothing personally,
least of all ourselves. For the moment that we do, our
spiritual growth and journey come to a halt.

The time of the lone wolf is over.

~A message from the Hopi elders

LETTING GO OF THE SHORE   LESSON 5

W̲e come to know ourselves when we are out of control. When we are in control, we are playing by rules and staying in lines not of our own making. We must be liberated, shackles off, to know who we are and what we are here for.

Through this process, we remember we have the power to see and reveal the underlying laws of nature. We realize we exist in an interwoven, connected reality, as if we are both the artist and the canvas.

Addiction carves out the space that God or spirit will inhabit. Then, when spirit pours in, it is not the superior rescuer, my-way-or-the highway form of spirituality, but the honest and grounded spirituality that can look at all things and say, "I am that," and, "Yes, even that, I am that, too." Even the muck and the mud.

Self-discovery occurs when we break free from constraints, allowing us to understand our true nature and purpose by recognizing the interconnectedness of reality. Embracing even our flaws and darkest moments, we can find a genuine spirituality that acknowledges and accepts all aspects of our being.

"To find your purpose, become lost."

~BAYO AKOMOLAFE

Meditation: Letting Go of the Shore

Introduction

Welcome to this guided meditation to let go of the shore and enter the flow of life. Just as a boat cannot move forward if it's tethered to the shore, we must release our attachments and fears to fully embrace the journey ahead. Find a comfortable, quiet place to sit or lie down, and let's begin.

Finding Your Center

Close your eyes and take a deep, cleansing breath in, then slowly exhale, releasing any tension or worries. Inhale again, deeply, then exhale fully. As you breathe, let go of the distractions of the day and bring your focus to the present moment.

Imagining the Shore

Visualize yourself standing on the shore of a tranquil, serene river. See the water gently lapping at the sand. The shore represents your comfort zone, the familiar, and the known. It can be limiting.

Letting Go of Attachments

One by one, bring to mind the things that limit you, your fears, your attachments. Place these attachments one by one onto the shore beside you. Visualize them lined up there. You no longer have to carry them.

Pushing Away from the Shore

Now, when you're ready, step into the water. Feel the gentle flow of the water as it holds you. Allow yourself to go deeper into the center of the river. You might feel a sense of apprehension or uncertainty, but that's okay. It's natural when embarking on a new journey. Surrender to the current as it carries you down river. Imagine the things you left behind growing smaller in the distance.

Entering the Flow

As you drift away from the shore, notice how the water beneath you is the flow of life itself. It's the current of possibilities, change, and growth. Feel the way the water holds you up as it guides you toward new experiences and opportunities.

Embracing the Unknown

As you continue to drift along the river of life, feel the sun warming your skin and a gentle breeze ruffling your hair. Embrace the unknown with an open heart. Trust that the current will carry you where you need to go. You are safe, and you are supported.

Surrendering Control

Release the need to control every aspect of your journey. Let go of the need for certainty and predictability. Surrender to the flow of life, and let it guide you toward your true purpose and fulfillment.

Affirming Your Courage

Take a moment to affirm your courage and your willingness to embrace the unknown. Repeat in your mind or out loud: "I am courageous. I am open to the flow of life. I trust in the journey."

Gratitude and Closing

Slowly bring your awareness back to your breath. Wiggle your fingers and toes, then when you're ready, open your eyes. Take a moment to feel gratitude for this opportunity to let go and enter the flow of life.

You can return to this meditation whenever you feel the need to release attachments and fears that hold you back. Embrace the journey. Trust that the flow of life will lead you to new adventures and personal growth. You are capable of navigating the currents and finding your true purpose.

Journal Exercise: Letting Go

- Take a moment to freely write about surrender. What is an area of your life that feels clenched, tense, or held tightly? How would it be to loosen your grip and surrender? What does surrender look like in this particular situation?

"For years, I was sure the worst thing that could happen to a nice guy like me would be that I would turn out to be an alcoholic. Today, I find it's the best thing that has ever happened to me. This proves I don't know what's good for me. And if I don't know what's good for me, then I don't know what's good or bad for you or for anyone. So I'm better off if I don't give advice, don't figure I know what's best, and just accept life on life's terms, as it is today — especially my own life, as it actually is."

~Alcoholics Anonymous: The Big Book

RE-ENTRY

LESSON 6

Hitting rock bottom is likened to a spiritual awakening, leading to recovery, yet reintegrating into society often involves pressure to renounce the nonrational aspects of our addiction experience. However, when we acknowledge the profound insights gained during addiction, we can achieve a deeper, more authentic connection with life and love.

W e can compare the concept of hitting bottom to enlightenment in traditional spiritual paths. This moment marks a turning point in one's journey, leading to the next phase, which is recovery.

Re-entry into the rational world can be a challenging process, as that world tries to demand we denounce our nonrational experiences and conform to the expectations of the rational world.

In other words, if we actually had a really beautiful experience in our addiction and we're now in recovery, people may expect us to slam our addiction experience and say it was awful. A common saying in recovery programs is, "My worst day sober is better than my best day using." But this is like dating someone who you're completely crazy about and then refusing to admit to dating them publicly, or denying it entirely later.

Those who return with courage and refuse to deny the beauty and profundity of their time in addiction will have gained a deeper understanding of intimacy with life, not from a position of superiority, but from a humble, nonrational standpoint. These individuals will have learned the mechanics of the human psyche from the inside, knowing how to exist without artificial boundaries and experience genuine love, and are unafraid to claim that. The invitation here is to hold all of the truth, rather than deny parts of it.

"Life breaks all of us but some of us get stronger in the broken places."
~ERNEST HEMINGWAY

Journal Exercise: You Are Me Too

- Reflect on who you became when you were in your addiction. How would you describe yourself before you knew addiction?

- In the midst of your addiction, who did you become?

- What did you discover about yourself that you didn't know was there?

Meditation: You Are Me Too

Think of who you became in the midst of your addiction when you went out of control. Who was that person? What parts reveal themselves to you? Looking at them, without judgment or shame, say to these parts, "You are me, too." And let them exist in you. Go to each one and allow it to reside in your heart. As you go through The Art of Addiction, you will learn to re-harness these parts of yourself into their evolved form.

At the end of the meditation, slowly bring yourself back into the room. Feel the seat beneath you and hear the sounds around you. Slowly open your eyes when you are ready.

"I realized today that well, I'm better because
I've gone through addiction, not worse."

~AOA participant

ALCHEMY

LESSON 7

We use the metaphor of alchemy to describe the transformative journey of turning personal adversities into growth and self-realization. Alchemy guides individuals through self-examination and healing to discover our inner fulfillment and purpose.

I n the Art of Addiction, alchemy represents the profound process of inner transformation and personal evolution. Much like the ancient practice of alchemy aimed to turn base metals into gold, psychological alchemy seeks to transmute personal challenges, emotional struggles, and inner conflicts into valuable insights, wisdom, and personal growth.

Alchemy is a powerful symbol of the human capacity to turn adversity, pain, and suffering into opportunities for healing, self-discovery, and positive change. It underscores the idea that within each individual lies the potential for profound transformation and the ability to find meaning and purpose in life's most challenging experiences.

In The Art of Addiction, we explore this concept by helping individuals examine their life experiences, confront their inner struggles, and work toward integrating and transcending them. Through this process, one can develop a deeper understanding of themselves, heal emotional wounds, and ultimately discover their own "gold"—a sense of fulfillment, authenticity, and purpose.

"Character cannot be developed in ease and quiet. Only through experience of trial and suffering can the soul be strengthened, ambition inspired, and success achieved."

~HELEN KELLER

Journal Exercise: What Have You Turned to Gold?

- While going through the workbook so far, you have likely been remembering and wrestling with certain parts of yourself. Free-write about which of these have alchemized for you.

- In what ways have they turned to gold?

Meditation: Alchemy

Close your eyes and take a deep, cleansing breath in, then slowly exhale, releasing any tension or worries. Inhale again, deeply, then exhale fully. As you breathe, let go of the distractions of the day and bring your focus to the present moment.

As you breathe, imagine each deep inhale is a warm, healing light. Allow this light to permeate the areas of your body where you've held onto pain. With each exhale, release some of the weight of your pain. Allow the rhythm of your breaths to bring you comfort and acceptance.

Discovering Wisdom

Now, envision the remaining pain transforming into a source of wisdom and strength. See it as a raw material, like lead, that has the potential to be transformed into something valuable, like gold. As you breathe, sense this transformation occurring within you.

Connecting to Purpose

Imagine a spark of light within your heart. This spark represents your purpose. See it growing brighter with each exhale. As you inhale, feel the warmth of this purpose expanding within you.

"The love I have for my life and my freedom is huge now. I can accept change and not run from it because I love myself today. I didn't used to...I know that it's okay because life is about progression, not revision."

~AOA participant

REFLECTION, INTEGRATION, AND CALIBRATION

LESSON 8

Love is about emptying ourselves of biases and embracing everything with hospitality, recognizing our own value as a prerequisite. It is a powerful force that challenges us to love unconditionally, transforming our understanding of ourselves and infusing all aspects of life.

The Art of Addiction can be used over and over to learn to love parts of ourselves that need to be refocused, harnessed, and loved. In this final lesson, you will answer questions and prompts that have you reflect on the previous lessons. Taking time to reflect on what you learned about yourself through this course will help you integrate these learnings into your life.

Journal Exercise: Getting to Know Your Parts

Let's go back to the list you made in Lesson 4 of the parts of your-self you wanted to let go of.

- Choose one of the items on the list and imagine it has its own thoughts and goals. Write down the item here:

- When you imagine this part of yourself, what does it look and feel like?

- Write down any thoughts, words, or images that come to mind.

- How does this part want to help you? What does it believe is its role? What does this part fear will happen if you let it go?

Meditation: What Needs Calibration Now?

Find a comfortable seat, whether it's on a cushion, chair, or directly on the floor. Close your eyes gently, allowing the outside world to fade away. Take a deep, cleansing breath in, then slowly exhale, releasing any tension or worries. Inhale again, deeply, then exhale fully.

As you settle into this present moment, bring your awareness to the gentle rise and fall of your breath. Feel the rhythmic flow, like the natural ebb and flow of life. Inhale deeply, and with each exhale, release any residual stress or anxiety. Let your breath guide you to a place of stillness within.

Now, turn your attention inward. Bring your focus to your heart center, the seat of your emotions. Ask yourself, "What needs calibration within me now?" Allow the question to resonate, like a soft echo.

As you continue to breathe, visualize a part of yourself that bothers you. Bring your attention to this part, without judgment or shame. Just notice it. With each breath, give it the space it needs to just be itself. Let it tell you what it needs to say. Listen without being critical.

Now, imagine a golden light growing within you. You are the director of that light. Shine the light onto that shadow part. Allow it to receive the warmth of your love. Give it all the love and attention it needs until it has room to evolve.

This may need to be done over and over as you grow your capacity to apply love, warmth, and softness to those places that have become hard and calcified.

Gently, begin to bring your awareness back to the present moment. Feel the ground beneath you, and when you're ready, open your eyes with a sense of renewed clarity and purpose.

Return to this meditation when you feel stuck, unmotivated, or held back by self-judgment.

Journal Exercise: How Can I Love This?

Love is the capacity to draw forth. This requires you empty yourself of all preexisting notions of who you are and what you're about, and get outside of the notion of right and wrong. When you do that, everything becomes love. It's important that to love, you find out who you are. Start by admitting your value, because until you admit your value, until you see your majesty just as you are, you're earning or you're proving or trying to get something. That's not love. That's a hustle. Love is offering; love is a fundamental hospitality and a welcoming of anything that walks through your door. Whatever it is, to the best of your ability, *welcome it*. What you'll discover is that love requires tremendous power. Cutting through the delusion that anything is unworthy of love takes power.

- Do you have the fortitude to love the most unlovable thing?

- Can you love that?

- Keep working with this question, "Can I love this?" When you're in relationship with love itself, things change. The notion of who you think you are and what you think you are dissolves. Love infuses everything, no matter the form it takes.

Journal Exercise

Revisit Lessons 4-6. Write down five things about yourself that came up during these lessons.

For each of these five things, ask yourself these questions:

- Can I love this?

- Why would I love this?

- Why would I give my love to something I view, or believe others view, as abominable?

- When something is hard for you to love, ask what is hard about it? Do you feel unsafe? What is it like? What does it neec?

- Begin to ask it questions and just keep following the questions. It wants to take you somewhere that it is hard. The place where it is hard is impacted love. It's not that there is lovelessness; it's that there is a knot of unexpressed love. You just gently go in there and ask it question after question. Think of it as scar tissue. These are places that have become hard and calcified from pain. That place or thing wants to love. If you stay persistent and practice loving those hard and difficult places, you'll become steeped in the love. Then loving that difficult thing becomes second nature. Write about what happens as you asked questions of the hard places.

Final Journal Exercise

As you complete this workbook, remember this is only the start of your journey. You may use this workbook over and over again.

- Make a list of parts of yourself that you would like to calibrate next. Choose one place to start.

CONGRATULATIONS!

YOU HAVE COMPLETED
THE ART OF ADDICTION COURSE!